From the Heart

A Children's Guide to Idioms in the Bible

Breaking Down Idioms Book #2

Written by Dr. Janielle Nordell, MD

Edited by Isaiah Nordell

Illustrated by Lauren Glass with Esther Nordell

Copyright © 2020 Dr. Janielle Nordell, MD

All rights reserved. No part of this book may be used or reproduced by any means, graphic, electronic, or mechanical, including photocopying, recording, or taping or by any information storage retrieval system without the written permission of the author except in the case of brief quotations embodied in critical articles and reviews.

Scripture taken from the THE HOLY BIBLE, NEW INTERNATIONAL VERSION®, NIV® Copyright © 1973, 1978, 1984, 2011 by Biblica, Inc.® Used by permission. All rights reserved worldwide.

Scripture taken from the KING JAMES VERSION (KJV): KING JAMES VERSION, public domain.

Scripture taken from the NEW AMERICAN STANDARD BIBLE®, Copyright © 1960,1962,1963,1968,1971,1972,1973,1975,1977,1995 by The Lockman Foundation. Used by permission.

Scripture quotations have been taken from the Christian Standard Bible®, Copyright © 2017 by Holman Bible Publishers. Used by permission. Christian Standard Bible® and CSB® are federally registered trademarks of Holman Bible Publishers.

Published by Kudu Publishing
ISBN: 978-950718-43-6

Dear parents,

Ever since publishing our first book, Isaiah has been absolutely obsessed with idioms. He has discovered that our entire world is filled with them. (Did you catch that one?) In fact, his sister Esther has also caught the idiom bug. While Isaiah continues to help with editing this second edition, Esther now helps with the artwork. I'm such a proud mama!!

Just like our everyday lives are full of figurative speech, the Bible is as well. We use idiomatic expressions constantly when teaching God's Word, whether in Sunday School, church, or in song. Many of us just fly by without realizing what such phrases would mean if taken literally.

Many of these idioms revolve around the heart. In fact, the Bible alone contains the word "heart" over 1,000 times. Why? The heart represents more than the organ responsible for pumping blood throughout the body. Most of us think about what the heart represents before even realizing that the heart is actually a vital organ.

Take a step back and try to think about some of our phrases with "heart." Can an actual heart have feelings? Of course not — our brain processes those. What about someone with a heart of gold — does it mean their heart is actually made of gold? That's ridiculous! How about "take heart"? If taken literally, one might imagine the notorious evil queen that steals her captive's actual heart to be in control of them. Gross. We could go on and on.

In order to grasp sayings of the heart, we first need to understand what the heart represents figuratively. In ancient times, the heart — not the brain — was believed to be in control of the body. The heart was responsible for both our physical and emotional well-being, in addition to being our moral compass. It is supposed to help us determine right from wrong. These attributes guide us in understanding what the Bible actually means when using the word "heart."

This book only starts to break down a few more of the idiomatic expressions found in the Bible. But don't lose heart — enjoy the journey as we explore God's Word together!

In Him,
Janielle

Esther created this work of art with all her heart. Find it throughout our book!

We dedicate this book to our cousins:
Sean, Cadance, Vida, Livie, Sven, Colton, Riley, Wyatt, Molly, Jackson, Cooper, and Colby. You are each beautifully made by God, amazing and uniquely wonderful in so many ways.

With love,
Isaiah, Esther Grace, Uncle Ben, and Tia J

As you make your way through this book, search for this hidden puzzle piece. The puzzle piece represents what started this adventure – helping children with autism better understand idioms. The heart and cross represent our hope to share God's love with everyone.

That is what this verse means. Your heart isn't actually in a treasure chest. We like to use the word "heart" to mean "love". We use a heart symbol to let someone know we love something or someone. When we treasure something, we love it a lot.

Proverbs 3:3 — Let love and faithfulness never leave you; bind them around your neck, write them down on the tablet of your heart.

Now this is crazy talk. How do you wrap love and faithfulness on your neck? Or worse, write them on your heart? I don't know about you, but my heart doesn't have a tablet.

The safest way to keep from losing something is to put it on a chain around your neck. But what about the "tablet" part? If you love somebody forever, we say that person is "in your heart". That is the same thing here.

If love and faithfulness are "written in your heart," then you remember to love others and always trust Him.

Proverbs 10:8a — The wise in heart accept commands.

Does this mean the word "wise" somehow gets in our heart? Of course not! Hearts pump blood, not words. The heart sends blood to the rest of the body, giving it energy to work right.

Psalm 34:18 – The Lord is close to the brokenhearted.

I know God is always close by me, even though I can't see Him. But what does "brokenhearted" mean? Can a heart actually break into pieces? No!

When somebody is "brokenhearted", they are sad. When you are sad, being with a friend helps you feel better. God stays close to people who are sad, just like a good friend does.

Psalm 51:10 — Create in me a clean heart, O God, and renew a right spirit within me.

Wait a minute. When you take a bath, do you also wash your heart to make it clean? No way — that's impossible! When we do wrong things, it is like we got our heart dirty.

This is just like when we need our dirty clothes washed after playing outside.

Jeremiah 29:13 – You will seek me and find me when you seek me with all your heart.

Is God asking us to play hide and seek with Him? No, but that would be amazing!

When you are looking for something, you use your eyes, not your heart. So what is this verse telling us?

A real heart pumps blood to give energy to our body. If you do something "with all your heart," you try as hard as you can, using all of your energy. God is telling us we will find Him when we do everything we can to look for Him.

God decides what is right or wrong. God says in the Bible to obey your parents.

By taking a cookie, he is disobeying his mom. That is wrong. When we obey God, then we know we are right.

Do you want to be strong? Me, too! But what do you think it means to "take heart"? Are we supposed to take somebody else's heart? No way! That would be horrible. When we say "take heart", you try your hardest not to give up.

Just like running a race, God gives you strength to finish. God is telling us to trust Him and to not give up.

Proverbs 28:14 — Happy is the one who is always reverent, but one who hardens his heart falls into trouble.

How can a heart be hard? Real hearts are soft because they are muscles that are always moving. Hearts can't do that if they are hard. Our hearts work best when they are soft — when we choose to do what is right. When a person "hardens his (or her) heart", they choose to do the wrong thing.

We should instead be reverent. This means you are careful to do what is right. When we choose to obey God, we will be happy.

Proverbs 17:22a — A joyful heart is good medicine.

When you get sick, you take medicine to feel better. Have you ever had medicine shaped like a heart? I haven't. When you are sad, how can you feel better?

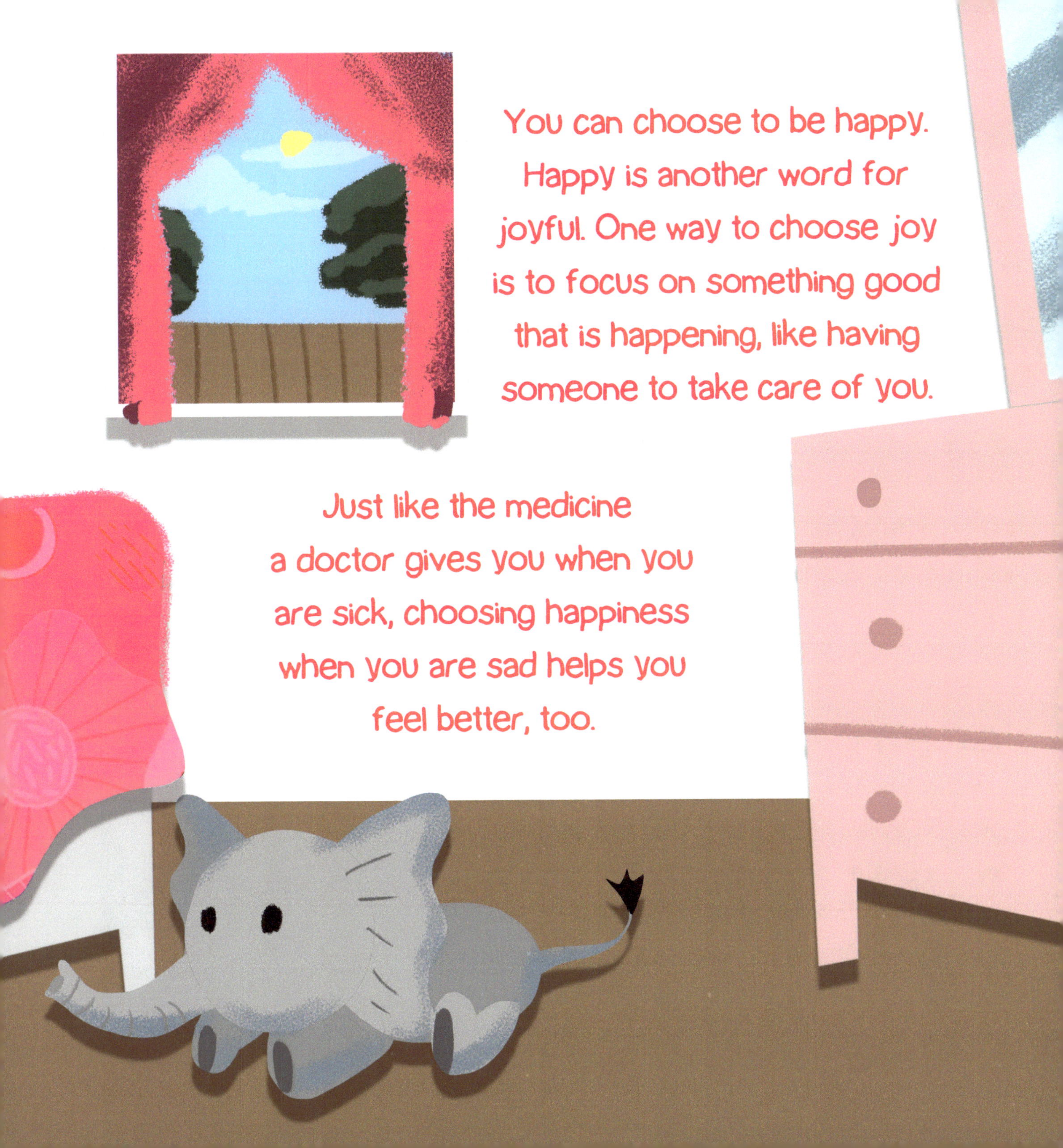

You can choose to be happy. Happy is another word for joyful. One way to choose joy is to focus on something good that is happening, like having someone to take care of you.

Just like the medicine a doctor gives you when you are sick, choosing happiness when you are sad helps you feel better, too.

ABOUT THE AUTHOR

Dr. Janielle Nordell is married and has two young children. Growing up, her family had a strong focus on mission work. They served in Ecuador, fueling her lifelong desire to care for the underserved as a pediatrician. She has been privileged to serve her community in Minnesota and overseas in Cameroon and Nicaragua. Her passion is to improve the wellbeing of all children. In her spare time, she enjoys writing children's books, playing the flute, learning to run, and taking on new arts and crafts.

ABOUT THE ILLUSTRATOR

Lauren Glass lives in North Carolina with her husband and son. As a former educator, Lauren values projects that benefit children and the community. She is so excited to be involved with this book!

www.ingramcontent.com/pod-product-compliance
Lightning Source LLC
Chambersburg PA
CBHW042133070426
42453CB00002BA/75